Flower
Arranging
through the year

Flower Arranging through the year

Daphne Vagg

B. T. Batsford Ltd.

First published 1983
© Daphne Vagg 1983

ISBN 0 7134 3732 4

Typeset by Typewise Limited,
Wembley, Middlesex
and printed in Hong Kong
for the publishers
B. T. Batsford Ltd
4 Fitzhardinge Street
London W1H 0AH

FRONTISPIECE
Mauve and pink roses with columbines and other
garden flowers in a simple basket arrangement.

Contents

Preface

Most of the photographs in this book first appeared in *The Flower Arranger* magazine, which has been published quarterly for over 20 years as the official publication of NAFAS, the National Association of Flower Arrangement Societies of Great Britain.

Colour was first introduced in the magazine in 1976, sending the circulation rocketing up to almost twice its previous figure in three or four years. It is now the largest-selling flower arrangement magazine in the world with a circulation of 45,000. Although it is available, post-free, to NAFAS members through their flower clubs, and by individual subscription direct from the printers, the magazine does not appear on bookstalls or at newsagents. Some of its excellent colour photographs deserve to be seen by a wider public, and with their aid this book takes readers through the seasons, looking at the different flowers, plants, events and opportunities which make up a flower arranging year.

Old-fashioned flowers in a Victorian box.

Arrangers and Photographers

53	Audrey Caldwell	Douglas Rendell
55	Daphne Vagg	John Vagg
56	Daphne Vagg	John Vagg
57	South-west Area, NAFAS	Douglas Rendell
58/59	Daphne Vagg	John Vagg
60	Joan Newlyn	B. Woodward Davies
61	Daphne Vagg	John Vagg

Introduction

You may think of flower arranging as a pursuit only for the summer months when colourful flowers are plentiful, but it can be an absorbing hobby all the year round, with interest in every season, as the pages following will show.

Since World War II thousands of men and women of all ages, and in every walk of life in town and country, have found pleasure in arranging flowers and have given pleasure to the many more who see the results. Some join flower clubs; some belong to their church flower guild; some are trained professional florists; some are gardeners first and foremost who bring their garden treasures indoors – and some are none of these things. They are just ordinary people who like to have a flower or two in the house for their colour or their scent.

It may be more than just a coincidence that, as homes have become centrally heated and open, living fires have decreased, the interest in flower arranging and growing houseplants has increased enormously. It is as though we all need to have something living, changing and growing in our rooms. Artificial flowers, especially the beautiful silk ones from the Far East, have their place (increasingly so in dry, centrally-heated atmospheres) but they have no life, they do not move or open from bud to blossom, and so they lack some of the greatest charms of fresh flowers.

We talk of 'flowers', but we mean also leaves, stems, berries, fruits, cones, seed-heads, bare

branches, bark and weathered wood. The so-called *flower* arranger uses all these, especially at those times of the year when flowers themselves are scarce or expensive.

Flower arranging is not difficult. It is much easier to do well, with only a little experience, than most other crafts. The potter has to start with an ugly lump of wet clay, the painter with mucky tubes of paint, the sculptor with unprepossessing blocks of wood or stone; but the flower arranger has a head start because what he or she uses is already beautiful in itself. It may not always be the conventional beauty of a rose or a lily; it may well be the colouring in a leaf, the curve of a branch or the rough texture of gnarled wood. With these the arranger composes a three-dimensional 'picture' much as the painter or sculptor might do, but using plant material.

There is a wealth of it available to most of us if we can only learn to see it. See it, that is, with an eye to its use as decoration, with an awareness of its colour, shape, line or texture and the possibilities of combining it with some other plant forms that contrast, complement, or echo the line, or repeat the colour, to create a new beauty. This development of the 'seeing eye', as it is often called, is one of the greatest joys of flower arranging. It is pure pleasure; as for the student who came to her fifth flower arrangement class in early spring, eyes shining, full of the news that she had found 'wild arum leaves growing by the dustbin!' They had probably been growing there, quietly multiplying, for untold years, but only now had she seen them and appreciated and enjoyed their black-spotted, elegant arrow shapes. With this kind of recognition comes the itch, the eagerness and sometimes quite overwhelming desire to be able to create something new.

There is no more joyful occupation than arranging flowers, and this book aims to show the varying beauty and interest that arrangers find throughout the year, the places where flower arranging takes them and the range of facets to the craft; I hope to tempt readers who have not already done so, to try their hands, to join a flower club, to offer to do the church flowers or simply to pick them for pure selfish pleasure.

LEFT An early spring arrangement uses the catkins of the alder tree which grows near water along river and pond banks. The little dark cones are also on the same trees, left from the previous year. Iris flowers from the florist and the lovely marbled leaves of *Arum italicum pictum*, a relative of the wild Lords and Ladies or Jack-in-the-pulpit, are arranged together in a modern footed bowl.

FAR LEFT Yellow, for most of us, is the colour of spring. Daffodils, yellow tulips and the sweetly scented sprays of *Mahonia japonica* flowers, with green hellebores and pussy willow, bring sunshine into winter-weary rooms.

OVERLEAF
Early mauve rhododendrons are grouped round a piece of rough textured wood on a hessian-covered circular base. There are two containers (both quite hidden so probably only tins), one behind and one in front of the wood. The apple-green flowers are those of the Corsican hellebore, and colourful polyanthus complete a massed arrangement.

11

Making a Start

Something to cut with is the only tool you will ever really need to start flower arranging. Start with the kitchen scissors. Later you may wish to buy special flower scissors and garden secateurs.

Containers

Because most plant material needs water to keep it alive, some kind of 'container' is required to hold the water and the arrangement. But it does not have to be the conventional vase, jug or bowl. Look through the kitchen cupboards for a sugar bowl, cereal bowl, casserole dish, sundae glass or sauce boat. Put a tin or a plastic dish inside a shallow basket or lidded box. Buy a candle-cup to fit in a candlestick. Later you can look for urns, antique containers or modern pottery to suit your own home.

Stem supports or 'mechanics'

The simplest way to put cut flowers in water is to stand them in a jug or vase, letting them settle where they will. Cutting the stems to different lengths helps to ensure that each flower can be seen and have its own display and breathing space. But, with this method, a variation in style is not easy, so a means to support the stems is needed. Then you can be sure that each stays exactly where you want it for your design and at the right angle. Today there are three methods frequently used:

1 A lead-based pinholder (also called a kenzan or needlepoint holder) is placed at the bottom of the container, held in place by putty-type adhesives such as Plasticine, Oasis-fix or strip Bostik. Stems are impaled in the pins and held firmly.

2 Wire netting (about 2-inch mesh) is crumpled to fit firmly into a container, giving several layers of supporting wire.

3 Plastic floral foams (such as Oasis, Bloomfix, Florafoam and Aquarius) are soaked with water and hold stems firmly in place. The foams can be cut to size and shape and either wedged into a container or supported by a pronged metal or plastic holder fixed, with putty-type adhesive again, to the container bottom. Stems can be held at any angle, even upside-down, and still drink the water.

A combination of methods is often used for large arrangements.

Conditioning

The other thing you'll need is a bucket or two for 'conditioning' the cut flowers and leaves.

Without water, most fresh-cut plant materials will quickly wilt and die. To replace the water supply they had in the natural state, put them into a bucket of deep water as quickly as possible. Leave them in a cool place to have a good drink for at least two hours, or overnight if possible, before arranging. They will then last well provided the water in their container is regularly topped up. Leaves can be soaked right under the water for two hours or so to make them really crisp and fresh.

A friend who arranges flowers can show you how to fix the mechanics and to 'condition'. Better still, go to a class, or join a flower club.

SPRING

CREATING A SCENE

Two designs using figurines show how much can be made of very little when flowers and leaves are scarce in early spring. On the right a classical lady stands beneath a curling, curving 'tree' of contorted willow *(Salix tortuosa)*. It was probably cut and brought indoors when the leaf buds were still tiny so that they opened out in the warmth of the house. One can do this with almost any budding branch in spring: hawthorn, flowering currant, forsythia, dogwood, all fruit blossoms, horse chestnut 'sticky buds', and pussy willow. It is one way of hurrying spring along, even with snow outside. The purple flowers are Lenten hellebores, first cousins to the Christmas rose *(Helleborus niger)*; so even in these first pages, one can see how very useful the hellebore family is in spring-time arrangements. The other design is very similar in style, but this was a show exhibit created by members of a flower club and the background stands nine feet high! The arrangers have created the atmosphere of a cool, breezy March day with a birch branch, rough wood, a few ferns and clumps of primroses and heather, set off by the dancing shepherd boy.

FIGURINES AND NARCISSI

As on the previous pages these arrangements both use figurines, but the styles are very different. They also both use narcissus flowers but, again, in a very different way.

This time the classical figure is the container and at the top of her column is a small bowl holding a block of floral foam as the 'mechanics'. The graceful crescent-shaped arrangement holds sprays of white spiraea (often called Bridal Wreath), narcissi, tiny daffodils and white-rimmed larger leaves which are from the hosta plant. These plants enjoy the shade and there are many, many varieties with different leaf markings.

This massed style of arrangement is usually known as 'western style' or traditional, in contrast with the one shown opposite which owes much to the oriental or Japanese style of arrangement known as Ikebana, where the important features are line, space and restraint in the use of flowers and leaves. As in the pictures on pages 14 and 15 a little scene is created here – with a carefully trimmed branch, pensive old man and narcissi clustered as they might grow. The water in the low dish plays an important part, creating a pool for the old man to sit by and the tree to bend over, as well as providing an actual water supply for the plants.

TULIPOMANIA

In 17th-century Holland people went quite mad about tulips, so much so that the obsession has come to be called 'tulipomania'. Huge sums of money changed hands as gardeners tried to acquire bulbs which would produce the desirable 'broken' or feathered colours. Many of the flower paintings by Dutch and Flemish Old Masters of that era include these valued tulips. The beginnings of the great Dutch bulb industry lie in this time.

Bulb flowers are easy to grow; they can even be grown indoors in a jar of water, as all the food the flower needs is contained in the bulb itself. There are many different types of tulips to choose from today, ranging from the tiny species for the rockery to the Darwin hybrids over two feet high, and from the shaggy, fringed Parrot tulips to the elegant slim lily-flowered type, or from the double peony-flowered blooms to the striped and streaked Rembrandts.

Arranged here in a low rectangular bowl filled with crumpled wire netting are 'Merry Widow' (pink edged with white), 'Jimmy' (cream) and 'Mauve Wonder'. The white lacy flower with them is laurustinus (*Viburnum tinus*) which flowers right through winter and spring. A great many of the dark green leaves have been snipped away to give a lighter, delicate look to the arrangement.

Buy tulips from the florist when they are still in bud; but they should have some of the petal colour showing or they may not open at all. A good way to tell if a bunch is really fresh is to see if the leaves 'squeak', as they should, when they are handled. Condition them by wrapping the bunch in newspaper and standing the whole thing in a bucket of deep water right up to the flower heads if possible.

18

INSPIRED BY AN OLD MASTER PAINTING

This arrangement was inspired by the Dutch flower paintings of the 17th century and includes a variety of spring flowers, such as tulips. The arranger has also used carnations, white narcissi, polyanthus, cowslips, wallflowers, grape hyacinths, cherry blossom, hellebores and lilies with bunches of grapes.

The large orange flower at the top is a Crown Imperial which has always symbolized the power and majesty of Christ. Each of the pendent orange bell-flowers is said to hold a tear because the plant failed to bow its head before the crucified Christ. Since then it has hung its head in penance. Towering above the lesser flowers, it can be seen in many a Dutch flower-piece. The shell included on the base is also frequently seen; it symbolized man's worldly wealth and possessions.

The splendid arrangements in the paintings never existed in actual fact. They were composed from notebook studies made by the artist when the flowers were in season and then incorporated into a painted bouquet when needed. The present-day arranger here will probably have used a large piece of soaked floral foam wedged into the urn. This will have enabled her to get that lovely down-flowing curve of flowers which leads the eye to the cluster of yellow cowslips at bottom left.

Similar arrangements can be made during summer and autumn. The secret is to have just one or two of many different types of flowers and to look for those with bending, curving stems so that there is a sense of movement throughout the whole design. It was easier for the painter; he could just draw a stem as he wished. The flower arranger needs to find a flower growing with just the right curve to the stem!

A CHURCH PEDESTAL

As late spring moves into early summer, the chestnut trees put on their cream or pinky-red candles of flowers. One does not often think of them as flowers for arranging, but in this church pedestal they have been used to great effect. The branches have been stripped of all leaves which would be too large and clumsy for such an elegant design. Most of the other flowers are from the florist or nursery-man and include lilies, stocks, gladioli and carnations. The jagged grey-green leaves are from the artichoke plant; the other heart-shaped leaves from *Hosta sieboldiana*. The soft pastel colouring of grey, white, cream, lemon and pink is sharpened by the addition of the darker red chestnut flowers.

Pedestal arrangements are especially popular in church because there is usually little furniture on which to stand a large arrangement and a column or stand can be placed almost anywhere it is needed, raising the flowers so that they can be seen from a distance. The column here is of alabaster and has a large bowl for the flowers securely tied on to the top. Often with such a large mass of flowers the arranger makes doubly sure of the mechanics by putting a large heavy pinholder at the back of the bowl to hold the tallest stems securely, with a block of foam in front and a cap of wire-netting over the whole container, firmly wired or tied to the pedestal itself. It may sound rather a 'belt and braces' affair, but it will all be hidden by the flowers and foliage; and there is nothing more heart-breaking than to have such a carefully constructed arrangement topple over in the middle of the sermon.

SUMMER

SHOW TIME

In May each year, the Royal Horticultural Society stages the Chelsea Flower Show in London. Inside the huge marquee, magnificent displays of flowers and plants are staged, mostly by professional firms and growers. In recent years NAFAS (the National Association of Flower Arrangement Societies) has taken a stand which is devised and set up entirely by amateurs – arrangers who are mostly housewives with no commercial sponsorship or backing to call on. A team of eight or ten, sometimes from far afield, undertakes the venture, hiring a van(s) to take all their props and flowers to London. They set up the display and then care for it, replacing flowers and topping up the water, for the four days during which Chelsea is open to the public. The picture shows part of the NAFAS stand in 1980 when the theme chosen was 'Inspiration of Colour'.

Each year also, but in a different part of the country each time, NAFAS stages its own Festival and Competitions, Britain's major flower arranging event of the year. Usually about 300 entries can be accepted in the competitive classes and there is invariably a ballot for places. In addition there are non-competitive displays, sales tables with every imaginable flower arranging aid, pottery, books, plants and accessories and demonstrations of flower arrangement by well-known arrangers. Most flower clubs, too, hold a show during the year, and many large county and agricultural shows include flower-arrangement classes in their flower tents. The Lakeland Rose Show in Cumbria, for example, has to have eight judges to cope with their 500 flower arrangement entries.

FLOWER ARRANGEMENTS THAT TELL A STORY

In flower arrangement shows today most of the competitive classes have titles, and the exhibitor is expected to interpret that title with the arrangement. So the container, flowers and other plant material, accessories, background and bases must be chosen specifically with the class title in mind. The judge will be looking not only for a well-designed exhibit with good plant material but also for how well the arrangement conveys the class title to the viewer. Seashore themes are always popular since most flower arrangers collect a few interesting shells, pebbles, dried seaweed curls, starfish, sea urchins or bleached driftwood to keep in their store of 'dry goods'. Used with carefully selected plant materials an interesting arrangement can soon be made.

The arrangement here was in a class called 'Neptune's Kingdom' and won first prize at a NAFAS Festival. Notice how cleverly Neptune's traditional crown and trident have been worked into the design; the crown is made from driftwood. Just one or two pebbles and a shell are used as accessories; they are not overdone. A large piece of driftwood forms the backbone of the design with dried foliage, shaggy chrysanthemums reminiscent of sea anemones and some blue-green leaves of hosta and sedum. It is always important that the plant material should tell the story without relying too much on accessories, though every piece in the exhibit should play its part in putting over the theme.

ONE TYPE OF FLOWER

In spite of all the clever things that can be done with flowers, there is still much pleasure to be had from a simple bowl or vase containing one sort of flower only. The arrangement of sweet peas is a lovely example. The arranger shows us the flowers in bud, and fully open, with the leaves and tendrils which are so characteristic of the plant. See how she has kept the creamy-white flowers mostly to the outside, to give a delicate airy outline, and has concentrated the deeper pinks towards the centre. The antique white china compote sets off the flowers perfectly. The lacy openwork base avoids all suggestion of heaviness. Almost any flower can be arranged with just its own kind, but some, like gladioli, for example, are rather stiff and difficult to arrange well.

Roses are always lovely; massed hydrangeas in pale tones of pink, mauve, blue and soft green look well, so do white marguerite daisies and dahlias. Daffodils never look better than when massed with plenty of their own green leaves, and the same is true of primroses and bluebells. Ranunculus and shirley poppies make vivid arrangements on their own and lilacs in dark and pale mauves, with most of their leaves stripped away, are impressive just arranged alone. Try to choose a container which complements the colour and the character of the flowers. Sweet peas need a glass or fine china container, roses look well in porcelain, boxes or baskets, while daffodils seem to call for a pewter tankard or unglazed pottery jug.

SUMMER PROFUSION

Picking just one kind of flower or a mixed bunch is a pleasure that owning even the smallest garden can give. The flat- or bedsit-dweller with only houseplants or a window box will find a mixed bunch less easy to acquire, though there may be a birthday bouquet or gift bunch from a gardening friend to arrange sometimes.

This mixed-colour group arranged in a turquoise-and-gilt Victorian lamp base is obviously from a well-stocked garden. There are blue and mauve hydrangeas, mauve and deeper purple clematis and their silky seed-heads (left of centre), deep pink roses, foxgloves, double pink poppies, pale mauve hosta spikes, orange lilies, honeysuckle and a spray or two of lime-green alchemilla tucked in to set off the brighter flowers. Although not identical either in colouring or in flowers used, the arrangement clearly echoes the flower painting in its wide gilt frame. The dark panelling is an excellent foil for both. The chief problems in putting together a group like this are to find some spikey and bell-shaped flowers to break up the many round shapes, and to balance the mixed colours. Choosing softer, greyed hues instead of bright reds and yellows helps a great deal.

DECORATING STATELY HOMES

One of the special privileges to be enjoyed in Britain is that of being able to visit so many stately homes and gardens. Flower arrangers are even more privileged when they take part in decorating one of these houses for a special flower festival. Usually the event is organized in aid of a charity, and the opportunity of working with flowers in beautiful surroundings is one the amateur arranger seldom refuses. There are nerve-racking hazards, of course. Priceless carpets and polished surfaces need to be protected from water spills, costly porcelain from accidental breakage and fragile embroideries from too rough handling, but the sheer aesthetic pleasure makes the anxieties worthwhile.

The organizers and designers are usually able to draw arrangers from a number of clubs in an area or county. Each club will pick its best arrangers for the task but usually try to include an up-and-coming, less practised member as a helper so that he/she will be able to gain experience. There is an overall design within which arrangers must work, and colours and even specific plant materials may be stipulated; but individuals will be able to create within those limits, choosing the best plant materials to enhance their feature of the house.

The picture is of an arrangement designed to complement a harp at Parham Park, Sussex. It is a fine example of a large display-piece in soft colourings chosen to harmonize with the room and the musical instrument. Most of the foliage, palm and pampas grass is dried, or preserved with a glycerine solution, which gives the beige-to-brown colouring. The creamy flower spikes are Bells of Ireland (*Molucella laevis*) carefully preserved. The lilies with their fresh green leaves provide a contrast in colour and texture.

CHURCH FLOWER FESTIVALS

Decorating churches throughout the year is a task happily undertaken by the arrangers of church and cathedral flower guilds. For special festivals designed to raise money, perhaps to restore the organ, roof or bells, it is often necessary to augment the number of arrangers with local flower-club members and others interested in 'doing the flowers'. These festivals have become an important feature in the last 20 years or so, staged in charming village churches, unprepossessing suburban ones and centuries-old cathedrals and abbeys throughout the land — including St Paul's Cathedral and Westminster Abbey in London. In 1981 arrangers came from all over the British Isles and from as far afield as New Zealand, South Africa and the USA to stage a festival at Westminster Abbey organized by NAFAS. The picture (right) shows displays in the South Transept interpreting some of the Guilds of the City of London whose badges are displayed on the panels. It was, of course, a group display with some half-dozen arrangers involved.

In complete contrast the smaller picture shows a very modern approach. A slender arrangement of white lilies with blue-painted leaves echoes the colouring and style of a simply embroidered modern cope displayed at Wells Cathedral during a flower festival there. Sometimes people find it difficult to get used to the idea of artificially colouring flowers and leaves, but here it seems more than justified since the particular blue-green of the cope panel is one rarely found in plant material.

SUMMER WEDDINGS

Although spring and Easter-time are usually considered the most popular times for weddings, any flower arranger who is involved with one will hope that it is to take place in summer. Even today, when white is less fashionable for brides than it was, most of them seem to prefer pastel colours, creams and whites for their flowers. For these no other season can really match the profusion of summer.

Neither of the arrangements here was actually used for a wedding, though the smaller one (left) was photographed specially for *The Flower Arranger* magazine to mark the wedding of Their Royal Highnesses the Prince and Princess of Wales in 1981. The arrangement included 'something old, something new, something borrowed, something blue'. The fresh flowers were new, the skeletonized magnolia leaves were old, the touch of blue is from tiny silk flowers and the gilded rosemary was 'borrowed' from an old Tudor wedding custom.

The pedestal arrangement in its wrought-iron arbour would grace any wedding, especially one with a marquee reception. The supporting figure is a fibreglass garden ornament (sturdy but lightweight) and the arrangement is a lovely example of delicate colourings, feathery grasses, roses, pale green and pink rhododendrons and the large pink spathes of anthuriums. Extravagant? Perhaps. But a wedding is a very special occasion when economy is not usually the first consideration.

ROSES, ROSES ALL THE WAY

The rose is possibly the one flower that everyone knows. Steeped in history, dedicated in the past both to the Virgin Mary and to Venus the goddess of love, it has never been out of favour. Certainly it is a favourite with all flower arrangers for its lovely form, range of colour and heavenly perfume. Nowadays we identify roses simply as 'large flowered' or 'cluster flowered' rather than by the older names of 'hybrid tea' or 'floribunda', but the variety of shapes, colours, names and sizes is still quite bewildering. Flower arrangers tend to like the subtler, off-beat colours of creamy-white, mauve-pink or apricot-buff, largely because they blend so well with other colours in an arrangement, as in the picture on the left of a prizewinner at the famous Lakeland Rose Show. The curious little green flowers are also roses, the quaint *Rosa viridiflora*, unspectacular in the garden, but always a talking point in an arrangement.

The other picture is of a prizewinner at the NAFAS Festival, 1982, in a class called 'Essence of the Rose'. Blooms in the pink-red range of colours are combined with rose foliage and lime-green alchemilla, a lovely foil to the pink colouring. At the base is a bowl of *pot pourri* made from sweet-smelling dried rose petals.

AUTUMN

AUTUMN COLOURS

The glowing colours of autumn are those of the turning leaves – yellow, orange, red and brown. We associate them with seed-heads, berries, ripe fruits and dry grasses.

This double arrangement in an antique coffee-grinder standing on a trivet and copper tray combines all these autumnal qualities. We can almost feel the warm, golden sun of an Indian summer as we look at it. The arranger has cleverly exploited an asymmetrical balance in the design by taking the dried grasses high up on the left-hand side, then leading the eye through the diagonal line of orange roses right down to table level in the lower arrangement. It is not an obvious 'look-at-me' line, but it is there if you seek it and holds the two parts of the arrangement together.

The other important features are the variety of plant materials and the subtle variations of colour within the autumnal colour scheme. No one type of plant actually *matches* another in colour. The dahlias are more orange than the single spray chrysanthemums, but not as vivid as the roses, there are several tones within the grasses and the greenish, immature 'Chinese lanterns' echo the green in the bunches of grapes. Perhaps better than any other container shown in the book, the coffee-grinder typifies the use of unusual things to hold flowers. Sometimes the container is needed only to hold the mechanics and the water and is quite hidden by the plant material. At other times it is, as here, a very important part of the whole design.

A BUNCH IN A JUG

People often complain that flower arrangers nowadays never use anything as simple as a bunch of flowers in an ordinary jug for their container, but this bunch of autumn flowers looks absolutely right in the simple, unglazed terracotta jug. It stands with a group of fruit and flowers on a wooden base.

For all its apparent simplicity, the arrangement is more skilful than it looks at first sight. Every flower is given its own breathing space and each one can be clearly seen, though they do not all face to the front and we can appreciate them in profile as well as full face. The side lighting throws shadows which model them three-dimensionally (see detail). The curve of the jug handle is truly part of the design, nicely echoed by the curves of the board used as a base. Crocosmia (montbretia) seed-heads top the bunch, with orange spray carnations (small ones with some half-a-dozen to a stem and available at florists all the year round), calendula, pink roses, a chrysanthemum, berries and two gerberas which are the large daisy flowers in the centre. Ripe fruits and some pelargonium leaves complete a glowing autumn picture enhanced by the gilt frame and rich colours of the picture on the wall.

As in the picture on page 38 the mixture of glowing but still-subtle colours is given much greater interest by the number of different tints and tones. Quite often arrangers try too hard to match all the oranges, yellows, blues or pinks and the result is flat and uninteresting even though shapes and textures may vary. Here the eye never really tires of looking from flower to flower, appreciating colour changes and harmonies.

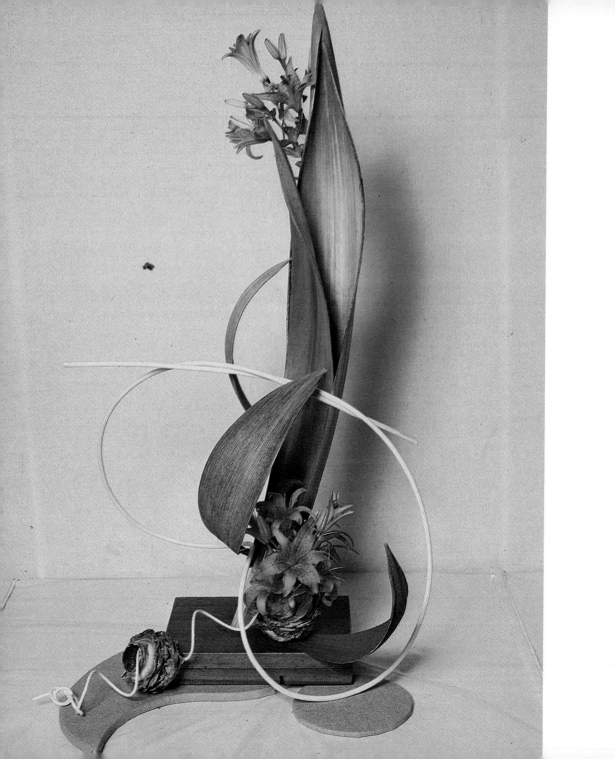

CUT-AND-DRIED

The description 'cut-and-dried' is apt for arrangements of dried plant materials, again with a few fresh cut flowers added. The dictionary defines it as meaning 'all ready, fixed or arranged beforehand' and that is what usually happens. The dried stems, leaves, spathes, seed-heads, wood or vines are contrived into an interesting pattern and then the colourful flowers inserted as accent features. For the most part such arrangements are sparse and therefore very modern in style, a far cry from the traditional massed groups of flowers. The emphasis is not on chocolate-box prettiness or formal beauty, but on interesting forms, intriguing textures and eye-catching lines with space used as an important part of the whole design. The effect on the viewer is stimulating rather than soothing.

The arranger has used curving coconut spathes (imported from abroad) a twist or two of white basketry cane and some cleverly shaped and covered bases to make the main structure. The fresh cut lilies were added with their stems in water, the top flower being held in a small tube fixed to the back of the tallest spathe.

For the busy arranger, this type of design has much to recommend it since a quick replacement of the flowers by another sort, or leaves or fruit, can alter the mood and atmosphere of the arrangement in a few minutes. It is very economical, too.

POT-ET-FLEUR

The term 'pot-et-fleur' (literally 'pot and flower') evolved, some 20 years ago, to describe an arrangement of growing plants (still rooted) with a few cut flowers. At times of the year when flowers are scarce or expensive a pot-et-fleur can provide a type of decoration which has never really enjoyed the popularity it deserves for its economy and long life. A well-planted and cared-for bowl will last for two or three years. Cut flowers can be added when they are available, and if they are not, then the plants alone are still decorative. Plants may be left in their pots, though this method may require an extra large container to hold them, or they can be taken out of the pots and packed into peat-based compost or sphagnum moss. Small pots or tubes are 'planted' at the same time to hold water for the cut flower stems. Depending on the size of the bowl, three to five plants are usually enough, with, say, three to seven cut flowers.

The pot-et-fleur pictured here is a very grand one – it was entered in a class entitled 'The Castle Gardens' at a NAFAS Festival. With so many rooted plants it needed a large, deep container, and the curve of weathered wood balances this well by giving height. The choice of plants for colour, shape, size and texture is most attractive, with the dark red colour arranged on one side and the cut stems of pink lilies flowing across to the other side to give perfect balance.

LOVELY LEAVES

We would never think to use the phrase 'foliage arranger', yet flower arrangers use leaves quite as much as they do flowers, perhaps more. Generally flowers are thought of as the stars of the show with the leaves as the supporting cast, but in the two arrangements here, foliage is featured in its own right.

The garland is an age-old form of decoration, going back to the ancient civilizations of Egypt, Greece and Rome. This foliage garland or swag in Rochester Cathedral used mostly lime-green sprigs of cypress, box, ivy, privet, skimmia and spotted laurel, but there are also pieces of red-purple berberis to provide a contrast in colour. What is essential, if the garland is to look attractive and not just a muddly green rope, is to get this variety of colour, shape and size in the leaves used. Garlands like this are usually constructed on long strings of 'sausages' of thin (dry-cleaner's) polythene wrapped round blocks of soaked floral foam or packed moss.

The other arrangement shows clearly the infinite variety of shape and colour in green leaves. The arranger has introduced the green seed-heads of poppy and phytolacca (also known as pokeweed or the red-ink plant) for greater variety and the large grey-green rosette is from the fleshy echeveria, usually grown in Britain as a greenhouse or house plant as it requires protection from frost in winter.

HARVEST FESTIVAL

At harvest festival time the vegetable, fruit and flower growers in the parish bring their gifts to decorate the church and chapel. Sometimes it is difficult to know how to use giant marrows, prize potatoes and massive onions and cabbages for the best decorative effect.

Here is an excellent way of making a large impressive display. A tall saucepan stand has been placed on a rush mat. Hessian or sacking would also be appropriate. Pieces of wire netting are laid on each shelf with one or two of the cut ends twisted round the stand uprights. Piling the larger vegetables on the floor, arrange the other fruits and vegetables attractively on the shelves, attaching them with wire or string when necessary. Then add cut sprays of berries and long-lasting greenery such as ivy (seen here with its flower clusters beginning to form into berries), cypress, laurel and rosemary. As with a pedestal of flowers there is the advantage that the stand can be placed where needed without cluttering the normal church furniture. We all too often ignore the decorative value of colourful fruits and vegetables, which have the added bonus that they can be eaten afterwards. Cabbages and marrows may not be your idea of a table decoration, but a smaller version of this stand using fruit and perhaps flowers would make an attractive display for a party buffet.

WINTER

IMMORTELLES

At first sight this arrangement of mixed flowers looks more appropriate to midsummer, and that, certainly, is when they were picked. But take another careful look. The photograph was taken in winter, and the flowers are all dried! What is more, almost all of them were preserved by the very simple method of hanging them upside-down in bunches for several weeks in a dry, airy place that is not too light (to prevent the colour fading).

To have this display in winter, one needs to harvest the flowers just as they reach their peak in the summer. All stems should be stripped of their leaves as these shrivel and are useless. The French word 'immortelles' is really more attractive than our own 'dried flowers' which always seems to suggest faded fustiness rather than a prolonged colourful existence.

Some of these flowers are annuals or biennials, which means they need to be grown from seed, or bought ready harvested, as they can be, from the florist. The blue delphinium spikes, feathery alchemilla and woolly grey heads of Lambs' Ears come up in the garden year after year. Once dried, the flowers are fairly brittle and need to be handled with care. If they are not to be used at once in arrangements, pack them gently into cardboard boxes (not in polythene which encourages sweating), and store the boxes in a dry cupboard or loft, not in a damp garden shed or garage, or the plants will soon be covered with mildew.

FAMILY HEIRLOOMS

Pictures made from dried and pressed flowers can sometimes be works of art worthy of being handed down as heirlooms to later generations.

Flowers and leaves for pressing are picked at any time of the year at whatever stage is needed. They are pressed in heavy books, in a press made or bought for the purpose, or sometimes under the carpet in the case of bracken or leaf sprays. They retain colour well but are, of course, flattened to paper thinness. You can dry flowers at their peak by hanging (see page 51) or by packing them in a desiccant such as sand, borax or silica gel. The flower or leaf retains its natural colour *and* its form. There are many books available which give details of both these techniques, and of preserving leaves and seed-heads with a glycerine solution – a technique which retains the form in a tough, pliable state, but changes the colour to a shade of brown.

The attractive pictures shown here are examples which use the flattened and the 3-D forms, taking the best from both worlds. For the most part the pressed plants are used to create the outline and 'bones' of the design, and the 3-D forms to build up depth and interest and to focus the attention. The muted colourings are among the greatest charms of this type of flower arranging. Preserve only what is in perfect condition and concentrate on the smaller flowers, leaves and seed-heads which are the most useful for pictures.

Even if you think an 'heirloom' may be beyond your skill, friends do appreciate greetings cards, calendars and gifts decorated with your own pressed flowers.

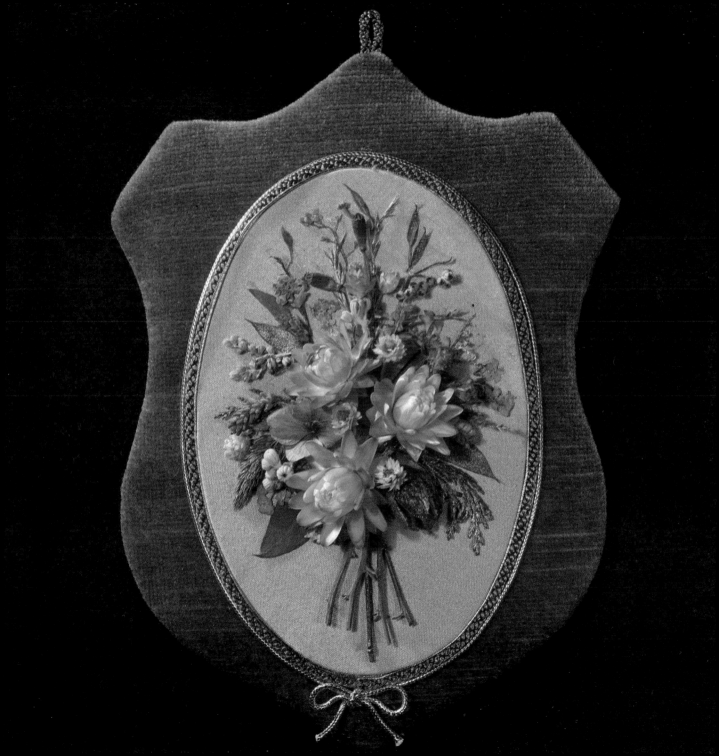

WINTER SUNSHINE

Here is another arrangement that looks like midsummer, but everything here is fresh and it was arranged in the second week in December with snow on the ground! The white flowers, of course, are from the florist, but are hardly an extravagance. They are just two sprays each of 'Bonnie Jean' and 'spider' chrysanthemums. The rest came from a snow-covered garden. The yellow leaves are from the holly 'Golden King', a gold and green variegated variety which frequently puts out shoots of all-yellow leaves. Clusters of white snowberries can be found growing in hedgerows sometimes, but these are a garden variety with bigger and more plentiful berries. The spikes of yellow berries are from another holly (*Ilex* 'Bacciflava') with all the plain green leaves stripped away. The seed-heads at the top are from crocosmia (montbretia).

Nothing here is very unusual, but it probably needed a flower arranger's 'seeing eye' to spot the possibilities of so summery looking an arrangement in midwinter. The off-white container is an inexpensive plastic replica of a classical urn and stands on a green mock 'marble' base. It would make a lovely table decoration for a winter wedding.

Any evergreen plant with white or yellow variegation such as ivy, periwinkle, euonymus, elaeagnus and the golden privet (which is not *quite* 'evergreen') will bring a touch of sunshine to a winter arrangement which plain dark green leaves can never do.

THE HOLLY AND THE IVY

In the Northern Hemisphere at least, Christmas is a time for the green and red of the holly and the ivy and if either of them has a touch of white or gold as well, then the Christmas colour scheme is complete. Both plants offer many varieties and cultivars with plain and lime green leaves and some with variegations of white, cream and yellow. All are easy to grow, not being fussy about soil, sun or shade.

Holly is slow growing, however, whilst ivy will root from almost any cutting and, once established, will romp away covering the ground, walls, fences, tree stumps and anything in sight.

Mostly, of course, it is the leaves we use for Christmas decoration, with the red holly berries as a bonus in the good years when they are plentiful – if we can get to them before the birds do!

The twisty wood in the picture on the left, however, shows another feature used by arrangers. It is actually a piece of ivy which grew over and around a rotten tree branch. Stripped of its bark (a long but rewarding task) it has dried to a mellow biscuit colour, and is arranged with sprays of several different ivies, three Super Star roses and the green, immature berries from a holly bush.

The striking red and green church arrangement complements a cope at Wells Cathedral, with holly and ivy foliage massed with red carnations to make a bold display. The gold and lime-green leaves effectively enhance the gold embroideries on the cope.

PARTY PIECE

It is probably only at Christmas and party time that most of us are prepared to accept flower decorations that are frankly fake, from start to finish.

We soon got tired, in the 1960s, of the cheap plastic flowers in rather garish 'natural' colours which were given away with almost everything from detergents to magazines. But the plastic flowers and foliage of recent years in shiny metallic or gleaming mother-of-pearl finishes are very different. So too are the ferns, leaves, berries and even flowers in turquoise, apricot, pink, lime-green and mauve. They are honestly unnatural and lend themselves to quite subtle colour schemes, but still with enough sparkle to suit our midwinter festive season.

This arrangement of material which is all artificial does not pretend to be anything else. The colours used are white, gold, pink and cerise, chosen initially to tone with the furnishings, but the arrangement could well be a party centre-piece with candles and napkins in a toning pink. The largest flowers are home-made from foil crepe paper with bead stamens, and the smaller ones from florists' waterproof ribbon. The pointed baubles are taped on to long dried stems.

Obviously, such an arrangement would not be cheap to buy all at once, so it is best to build up, each year, your stock of plastic and homemade materials so that you acquire a store to choose from. They last for years so it is a good decorative investment. Simple ribbon or paper flowers are easy to make, and can be the exact size, shape, colour and length of stem that you need. They can be prepared well in advance of Christmas or the party leaving you free to concentrate on last-minute jobs.

CHRISTMAS CANDLES

For most of us, our Christmas decorations will be in the traditional red and green, with touches of white and gold. The tall three-tiered arrangement (left) can be constructed on a dowel rod set in plaster-of-Paris in a large flower-pot saucer. Oasis-packed wreath rings can be used for each of the circles. Short sprigs of holly are pushed into the soaked Oasis, and if berries are scarce, looped ribbon bows can be used to provide colour. Bells hanging from ribbons give another festive touch. The candles at the top could well be real, but in this case they are red-dyed bulrushes. Standing at the foot of an angled staircase, it gives a cheerful welcome to guests as they enter the front door.

For the dining room sideboard, chest in the hall or cupboard top, two fat red candles are placed at unequal heights and flanked by two containers (right), one slightly raised and the other flat on the red oval base which unites the whole group. Red gladioli and carnations, tan-coloured single chrysanthemums, a pineapple, golden privet, rosemary and spotted laurel leaves are arranged to look as one design.

The year is almost at an end. When the festive season is over and the New Year has been welcomed, it is time to look forward and to bring indoors the alder catkins and horse chestnut 'sticky buds' to hasten the spring along and savour each season all over again.

How and Where to Learn More

Flower clubs

If you would like to learn more about flower arrangement, join a flower club. With nearly 1300 such clubs all over the British Isles and in many other countries all over the world, there is probably one much nearer than you think.

The National Association of Flower Arrangement Societies (NAFAS), 21a Denbigh Street, London SW1V 2HF (tel: 01-828 5145) will be pleased to put you in touch with your nearest club or local secretary.

Meetings are generally held once a month and last about two hours. There is usually a demonstration of flower arranging by a visiting expert, or a talk, or a practice session. Members hear what other flower-arranging events are taking place locally and nationally; they can buy arranging aids and accessories at reasonable cost; order *The Flower Arranger* magazine; borrow flower arrangement and gardening books from the club library and perhaps buy plants or preserved plant materials brought by other members. In addition they meet others with similar interests and that inevitably leads to new friendships and greater involvement.

Classes

Classes in flower arrangement, both day and evening, are available at many adult education centres. Some run a once-a-week course extending over one or two terms or short courses for five or six weeks. One-day workshops may also be available. These classes will be run by the local education authority. Enquire at your local library or ask at the nearest adult education centre.

Longer, and more intensive courses, both in flower arrangement and floristry, are provided at many colleges of further education. These generally lead to a City and Guilds of London Institute examination which gives a recognized national qualification to those who pass. The flower arrangement course is a three-year one, taken on one day a week, and besides practical flower arranging it includes botany, horticulture and design.

Training for a career

Generally speaking flower arrangers are amateurs, though some, of course, receive a fee for teaching, demonstrating or judging. Not many actually earn their living by arranging flowers. They do it because they love it and it is their hobby. Florists, on the other hand, are trained professionals who earn their living through arranging flowers. If you think you are interested in a career in floristry, then consult a florist near you or contact The Society of Floristry; the Secretary is at The Old Schoolhouse, Payford Bridge, Redmarley, Glos.

Suppliers

Any selection of names and addresses must be largely personal, but if you do not know where to begin, the following will get you off to a good start.

Flower-Arranging Tools and Equipment

Flora Products Mail Order, Stanley Gibbons
   Magazines Ltd., Drury House, Russell Street,
   London WC2B 5HD
Local florists and garden centres
Flower club sales tables
Stalls at larger flower arrangement shows

Seeds

If you plan to grow your own flowers, then the cheapest method is from seed. Garden centres, supermarkets, chain stores and DIY shops often have very extensive displays of packets. The alternative is to send for a seed catalogue (usually only for the price of the stamp) from one of the large seed firms such as:

Suttons Seeds, Torquay, Devon TQ2 7QJ
Dobies, Llangollen, Clwyd LL20 8SD
Unwins, Histon, Cambridgeshire

Flowers

Most towns have at least one or two florists' shops where cut flowers and house plants can be bought. Nowadays they also carry a selection of artificial 'silk' flowers, though many are actually made from polyester. Garden centres may also have cut flowers for sale and so do many nurserymen and specialist growers, though often they only cut for special orders.

To send flowers as a gift some way away you need to find a florist who displays the 'Interflora' or 'Teleflorist' sign. They will order flowers for you by phone and the florist nearest to the address where you want the flowers sent will deliver them. This is often possible the same day if the order is placed early. According to the price you pay, the flowers go as a simple bunch or already arranged in a container, or you can choose a houseplant or planted bowl. The florist will have pictures of typical arrangements and plants for you to look at. Naturally the service is not cheap, nor will you be able actually to choose the flowers yourself; but you can order certain flowers and particular colours and a message can go with them.

Herbaceous plants

Garden centres and nurseries are the best local sources, but if you need something special send for these catalogues:

Bressingham Gardens, Diss, Norfolk
Beth Chatto, Elmstead Market, Colchester, Essex

Bulbs

Most of the usual ones can be bought locally at garden centres or chain stores, but if you fancy trying some of the less usual bulbs or varieties, then get a catalogue from:

Blom's Bulbs, Coombelands Nurseries,
   Leavesden, Watford, Hertfordshire WD2 7BH
Van Tubergen, 304A Upper Richmond Road
   West, London SW14 7JG

Roses

R. Harkness & Co Ltd, The Rose Gardens,
Hitchin, Hertfordshire SG4 0JT
E.B. LeGrice Ltd, North Walsham,
Norfolk NR28 0DR
John Mattock Ltd, Nuneham Courtenay,
Oxfordshire
Wheatcroft Roses Ltd, Edwalton, Nottinghamshire

Trees and shrubs

Hilliers Nurseries, Amplefield House, Amplefield,
Romsey, Hampshire.
Notcutt's Nurseries Ltd, Woodbridge, Suffolk

Lastly, though really they come first and foremost among the suppliers, are your friends, gardeners and other flower arrangers. I have never met one yet who was not generous with seedlings, rooted cuttings and pieces from a divided plant. There is a phrase which says 'admire to acquire' and it has seldom been known to fail. Many gardens are full of snippets and roots from friends. 'Peggy's ivy' or 'Helen's periwinkle' or 'Mr Brown's hosta' are all the more precious for their associations and the willow grown from a cutting from 'that big demonstration at Brighton' recalls a very special occasion. And, what is more, they were all free. Flower arranging as a hobby is full of pleasures like that.

Index